Thomas Edison

✸

Genius of the Electric Age

D0910990

Published by VIZ Media, LLC, a member of the Shogakukan group
San Francisco, CA, the United States of America
Published simultaneously in Canada
Printed in Canada
First Edition, September 1, 2011

For information about permission to reprint any portion of this volume, write to:
Permissions, Shogakukan, VIZ Media, LLC, P.O. Box 77010
San Francisco, CA 94107

ISBN: 978-1-4215-4237-9

Book design: Koichi Hama
Translation: Molly Des Jardin
Copy Editing: Alan Gleason
Coordination: J-Lit Center
Supervision: Shiro Yamakawa
DTP: Showa Bright

Shogakukan Biographical Comics, VIZ Media, LLC,
295 Bay Street, San Francisco, CA 94133

Thomas Edison

Genius of the Electric Age

Tetsuya Kurosawa
writer

Tatsuyoshi Kobayashi
illustrator

Shogakukan

Thomas Edison
Table of Contents

Main Characters

Thomas Alva Edison
The "king of invention," born in Milan, Ohio

Samuel
Edison's father

Nancy
Edison's mother

Mary
Edison's wife

Francis Robbins Upton
Edison's assistant and master mathematician

Franklin Leonard Pope
Edison's telegrapher friend

Frank Jehl
Edison's assistant

Henry Ford
Edison's close friend and "king of the American automobile", organized the 50th anniversary celebration of the electric light bulb

Alexander Graham Bell
Edison's rival in the "telephone war"

J.U. MacKenzie
Edison's telegraphy teacher

Prologue: Reappreciating Edison

Yeah, it's a book report.

So I've got to read a book tonight. Bummer!

There's this movie I want to watch on TV, but ...

Yeah, I know.

It really stinks.

Daisuke, are you still on the phone?!

Uh oh! It's my mom!

Gotta go.

The lights aren't even on.

BLINK!

Okay, okay.

Gotta do it. Guess I better start reading.

We take it for granted that we can talk to our friends far away, with the lights on at night, surrounded by music.

Did you know that this easy life of ours is thanks largely to the ideas of just one man?

His name was Thomas Alva Edison.

Edison invented many of the things we can't do without in our modern life ...

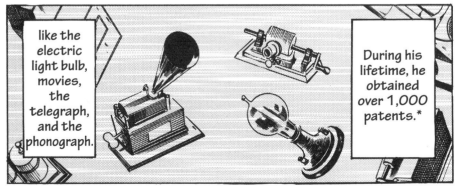

like the electric light bulb, movies, the telegraph, and the phonograph.

During his lifetime, he obtained over 1,000 patents.*

*Patent: the right of an inventor to be the only one to make and sell his invention.

Edison was truly the king of invention, but what kind of person was he?

Surely he got top grades in school, and was so rich that he could spend all his time inventing?

But no — he was nothing like that!

1862: Port Huron, Michigan

Chapter 1: The Young Publisher

Whoa! The train's already here.

Hurry up, mister!

Here it is, Al.* Today's paper.

Take it.

*Al: Edison's childhood nickname.

"The Battle of Shiloh* has begun.
What will be the outcome of the showdown between Union
General Grant and Confederate General Johnston?"

What an amazing battle.
This is big news!

Mister,
give me another
100 papers.

What on
earth for?

I'm going
to
sell them,
of course!

*Battle of Shiloh: a major battle during the Civil War (1861-1865).
Shiloh: a place in southwestern Tennessee.

11

*Telegraph: a way of transmitting messages long distances using electricity.

Al, you're getting on that train, aren't you? Hurry up or you'll miss it!

Oops! Gotta go!

Edison made sure that every station got a telegram with the day's newspaper headlines.

Wow!

There's a whole crowd!

Hey, it's about the Battle of Shiloh.

Who's winning?

13

Hey, everyone!

Wanna buy a newspaper with all the latest news about Shiloh?

A paper?

Ha ha! Good timing!

I really want to know more after seeing that headline!

Give me one!

Me too!

Hey, over here!

Because of Edison's idea, the newspapers sold like hotcakes.

No pushing! No pushing!

With the money he made from selling papers, Edison was able to buy a second-hand printing press and start printing his own newspaper.

I did it. I've got my very own paper!

Papers here! Edison's newspaper!

All the news in town, for only 8 cents!

Well, well!

Hey, it's even got the train schedule.

This is great!

One, please.

15-year-old Edison's newspaper made quite a splash.

Even The Times* of London wrote about it.

Edison's newspaper, The Weekly Herald

*The Times: England's most famous newspaper, established in 1785.

I wonder if it'll work ...

This is Al. Over. Over.

In 1835, Samuel Morse launched a new era of communication with his invention of the telegraph and Morse code.

Samuel Morse

By using a code of dots and dashes for the letters of the alphabet and converting these into electrical signals, Morse created a way to send messages long distances in an instant.

Morse Code

a • —	h • • • •	o — — —	v • • • —
b — • • •	i • •	p • — — •	w • — —
c — • — •	j • — — —	q — — • —	x — • • —
d — • •	k — • —	r • — •	y — • — —
e •	l • — • •	s • • •	z — — • •
f • • — •	m — —	t —	
g — — •	n — •	u • • —	

Example: — • •   — — —   — — •   → dog

It was a great invention, as significant as the computers, fax machines, and Internet of today.

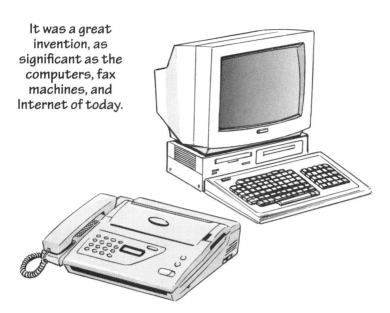

A reply!

TAP TAP

Edison had connected an electric wire to his friend's house 800 yards away,

and sent messages with the telegraph he had made.

19

Al, are you still awake?!

What time do you think it is?

URK!

Oh, hi!

Look at this, Dad. I finally got my telegraph working!

But ...

Never mind that, get to bed!

I just got a newspaper article from my friend.

There's a big sale tomorrow

at Marco's!

Really?!

In that case, I'll have to go buy some lamp oil!

That telegraph is really handy!

Yup!

Did you make it yourself, dear?

Not again!

You're just spoiling him.

Come now. Let's go downstairs and have some coffee.

Be in bed by midnight, Al.

Thanks, Mom!

21

I can't believe that boy.

Who does he take after, anyway?

First he's selling newspapers,

You put up that strange tower in the yard and went looking for customers.

and now he's sending telegraph messages all night. He's always doing something odd.

Now, isn't that just like you, dear?

I mean, just recently...

Strange tower? That was a grand observatory!

It's already been 15 years since Al was born.

Tee hee! Still, time certainly flies, doesn't it?

So it has.

WAAH! WAAH!

It was a cold winter day. The snow was dancing in the wind outside.

WAAH!

WAAH!

Look, Nancy. What a big head he's got!

But ...

he has such wise eyes.

On February 11, 1847, Edison was born in Milan, a small town in Ohio.

When Edison was 4 years old ...

Hey, Papa. Why do geese lay eggs?

If people keep them warm, will they hatch?

Why don't people lay eggs?

Ha, ha. There he goes again!

Al and his "Why? Why? Why?"...

Al, we've got work to do.

Eggs should hatch no matter what keeps them warm.

Huh ...

When Edison was a boy, he was interested in everything. He did nothing but ask questions day and night.

And he never tired of trying out new things.

OH NO! AL!

Oh my! He's really trying to keep the eggs warm.

Hmm ...

So this is where they store the wheat.

Because of this, he often got into trouble.

Huh?

I wonder what this handle's for.

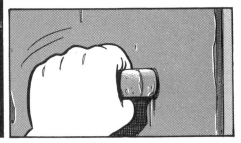

AUGHHH!

FWOOSH

Help! The kid's buried in the wheat!

Edison caused his parents all kinds of trouble.

I don't know what's gotten into him.

We're so sorry.

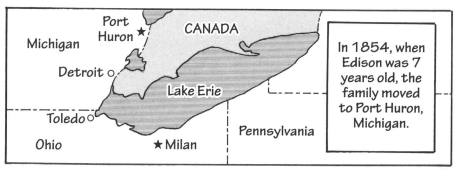

Michigan

Port Huron ★

CANADA

Detroit ○

Lake Erie

Toledo ○

Ohio

★ Milan

Pennsylvania

In 1854, when Edison was 7 years old, the family moved to Port Huron, Michigan.

In 1855, Edison started school.

It was so small it was hardly a school — just the pastor and his wife teaching in the church.

So, two apples plus two apples make four.

Got it?

I've got a question, sir!

What if they're green apples and red apples?

Here we go again ...

29

You've got to do something about Alva, Ma'am!

His questions are disrupting the whole class!

But ...

How could asking questions be bad?

What ?!

Isn't that a teacher's job — to answer questions?

Alva's questions have nothing to do with the lessons.

But it's still important to answer them!

31

Edison read all kinds of books with his mother ...

Gibbon's *Decline and Fall of the Roman Empire,* Hume's *History of England,* and *The Works of Shakespeare,* to name a few.*

Among these, Edison's favorite was

a science textbook, Parker's *School of Natural Philosophy.*

He tried out the book's experiments in his own basement.

Day after day, always experimenting.

Don't you think it's a bit too much?

Not at all. Let's let him pursue his interests.

32

The Decline and Fall of the Roman Empire, The History of England, and *The Works of Shakespeare* were famous books and plays written between the 16th and 18th centuries.

LURCH

ACK!!

That was close!

It's pretty shaky when the train's moving.

But after a fire broke out, he was forced to close his lab.

RATTLE

RATTLE

Even after he started selling newspapers, Edison set up a lab in the baggage car of the train.

One day in 1862 ...

Good morning, Mr. MacKenzie!

Mount Clemens, Michigan

Can I look at the telegraph again?

Sure, Al. Go ahead.

Ha, ha. That kid really loves the telegraph.

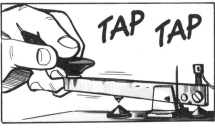

TAP TAP

Al, don't you have papers to sell?

Yeah. But it takes time for them to hook up the boxcars.

Well, Jimmie...

It's hot out. Let's go inside.

34

RATTLE

Jimmie! Al!

Are you both all right?

Al, thank you!

You saved Jimmie's life.

If there's anything you ever need — anything at all ...

That's right! You love the telegraph.

I'll teach you how to use it!

Wow!

Really?!

From the very next day, Station Master MacKenzie began teaching Edison the telegraph four days a week.

That's it.

A real telegraph.

Edison began studying telegraphy night and day,

making remarkable progress in a short time.

Chapter 2: The Young Telegrapher

In April 1864, through the introduction of Mr. MacKenzie, the Mount Clemens station master,

17-year-old Edison became the night telegraph operator at Stratford Junction, Canada.

Oh, no!

I dozed off again.

OW!

Wh-what?

No response from Stratford Junction?

We're getting the hourly signal ...

but when we send a message there's no reply.

Something must have happened. Send someone over to check on it.

Hey, Edison!

Are you okay?

ZA..

What's this?

CLICK CLICK

The telegraph is moving on its own

and sending signals!

Hey, Edison, wake up!!

What on earth is this?

Huh?

Oh, that — isn't it great? I made it myself.

It's a device that automatically sends a signal every hour.

43

Wow, that's certainly handy.

Whoa — What were you thinking, you idiot? This makes the hourly message meaningless!

URK!

This was Edison's first invention.

After that, he left his job and began a period of aimless drifting.

The Civil War was still in progress, but with his qualifications, Edison always managed to find work.

45

Why don't you take the New York Number One line?

Th-the Number One!

Edison, the New York Number One is the easiest line here.

If you can't handle it, you're not cut out to work here.

Got it.

I'll do my best.

Hey! The New York Number One ...

He'll be up against the fastest operator in America!

CLICK

Something's coming in!

Whoa!

Okay!

TAP TAP TAP

Hey, what's he typing?

He's going too fast to read it.

"Are you typing with your feet?"

Heh heh.

I've never seen anything like it!

YEE-HAW! Check out the new guy! He's the fastest gun around!

?

?

Sometimes, in his spare time ...

Edison soon became known as the fastest operator in the nation.

Success!

We got the cockroach in one shot!

Did it work?

Edison's "cockroach extermination device"

was made of two strips of tin foil with an electric current running through them, which would electrocute any cockroach crossing the strips.

You did it, Edison.

You're a genius!

But with a knowledge of electricity, anyone can make this.

I want to make something much greater!

What do you mean, greater?

49

Edison began to worry about what he should do next.

The State Legislature is hopeless! If they take this long to vote, no law of value will ever get passed.

Fellow voters!

Hmm.

What do I really want to do with myself?

At that time, Boston was the center of new technology in America.

It was full of young people who were excited about inventions and wanted to study the latest technologies.

Hm?

Wow!

A new telegraph machine!

That's nothing.

I could improve that thing so it would be much easier to use.

I-improve it?

You're a telegrapher too?

Heh heh.

I'm thinking of something much better than the telegraph.

Better than

the telegraph?

I can't say too much right now,

Oops! Gotta go.

Time to get back to the shop.

but when I'm finished the telegraph will be history.

My name's Graham Bell.

You'd better remember it. Someday you'll hear that I'm the greatest inventor of the century.

This very young man later became Edison's rival in developing the telephone — Alexander Graham Bell.

At the time, Bell worked at a fire alarm company in Boston and had already begun research on the telephone.

Alexander Graham Bell

An inventor ...

That word, "inventor," captured the anxious Edison's heart. He saw a glimpse of his future.

Inventing — that's what I've been doing all along!

If I could make it my life's work, what could be better than that?

So if voting in the State Legislature takes too much time ...

And so Edison produced an electric vote-recording machine.

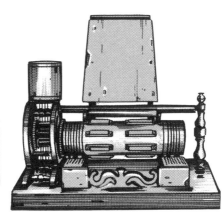

In June 1869, patent #90646 was registered. It was Edison's first patent.

Massachusetts State
Legislature
Office of the Speaker

An electric vote recorder?

Yes.

"Yes" and "No" buttons are installed at every representative's desk,

and you can view the results of a vote right at the Speaker's podium.

On top of that, it will record the result on paper.

YES

NO

Huh, imagine that. How convenient!

Isn't it?

But ...

we can't use it.

What?

B-but why? Didn't you just say it was convenient?

If you used this, voting could be completed in an instant!

Listen, son.

You simply don't understand politics.

Huh?

Our democratic government is based on majority rule, as you know.

So how do parties with only a few members

take on those in the majority? Do you know?

We win!

No ...

They make sure voting takes a good long time.

That way, time runs out and a decision by vote has to be put off.

Your device really is something.

But it simply isn't needed.

......

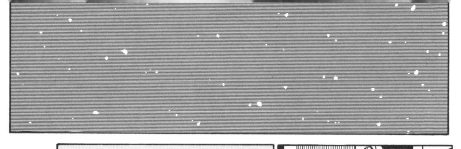

Edison described his day at the State Legislature to his friend Pope.

TAP TAP

Edison had friends all over the country through the telegraph.

... So that's what happened. My debut was a total failure.

I see ...

How terrible. Al's invention was rejected ...

Franklin Pope worked at a New York company that used the telegraph to send the latest information on the price of gold to its customers.

Well, what will you do from here on, Al?

TAP TAP

I have no idea. I used all my savings, so I can't invent anything for now.

In that case, why don't you come to New York?

New York?

TAP TAP

Yeah, Al!

New York is the very heart of America. It's the American Dream, Al!

The American Dream ...

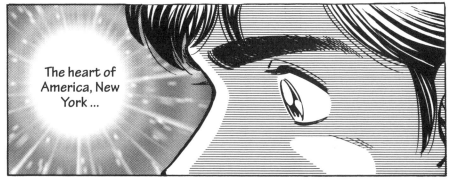

The heart of America, New York ...

58

That's it!

In New York, I can become somebody!

Edison sold all of his belongings and set out for New York.

Chapter 3: The Road to Great Inventions

May 1869: New York

HA HA HA!

Slow down, Al. Your dinner's not going to run away!

But Pope,

Okay, next, I'll show you to your lodgings.

I haven't eaten in three days!

Lodg-ings?

So, how do you like it?

It's the cheapest place you'll find in New York.

By that, I mean it's free.

It's the basement of my company. Doesn't get much light, I admit.

But until you get yourself set up, you can stay here.

Pope.

I can't thank you enough.

Heh!

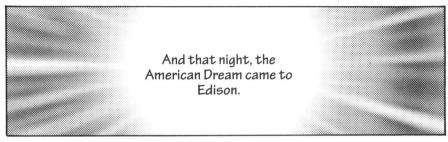

And that night, the American Dream came to Edison.

Come on, hurry! Do they know the cause yet?

This is awful! They're having a fit on the trading floor.

Huh?

AUGHHH! We've got to fix it now —

or our company's done for!

What's going on, Pope?

Oh, it's you, Al.

The gold price ticker broke!

Where? Show it to me.

Hey, what are you doing?

Hmm ...

If this works like that ...

Aha!

Yeah, that's it.

Look.

There was a screw stuck in there.

Boss, it's started up again!

It's all right now!

Wow!

63

Amazing! Do you work here, young man?

Ah — No, sir.

My name is Edison. I'm staying in the basement for a while.

Actually, I'm unemployed right now ...

No problem. From now on, you're working for me!

Are you serious?!

And so Edison came to work on improving the gold price ticker for the company.

The gold market exchange was a way of making a profit by buying and selling gold according to its changing price.

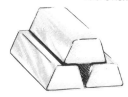

Edison improved the price ticker, and in August and September 1869 he obtained two more patents.

The gold price ticker was a type of telegraph used to quickly send the price of gold to the traders.

Gold price ticker

For a while the days went by smoothly, but one day ...

Al, I've got bad news!

The president sold our company to Western Union!

WHAT?!

What should we do, Al?

......

Edison! Pope!

Won't you stay on with us? I'll pay you double your salary.

The President of Western Union, William Orton

Thanks for the offer, Mr. Orton. But we're done working for others.

We're going to set out on our own.

Edison founded his own invention company.

It was 1869, and Edison was just 22.

He turned out one invention after the other. In 1869, it was his improved gold price ticker: the Gold Printer. In 1871, he produced the Edison Universal Stock Printer, which included a forerunner of the first electric typewriter.

Edison Universal Stock Printer

Edison's inventions were quickly bought up by big companies.

Finally! My own shop!

In 1871, Edison built his own factory in Newark, New Jersey.

"My dearest Mother,

How are you feeling? I hear you haven't been well. I've finally set up my own shop. Once I'm settled in, I'll come home for a long visit."

But on April 9 that year,

Edison's beloved mother fell ill and died before he could return home.

Ahh! If only ...

If only I'd come home sooner ...

Mother ...

Crushed, Edison returned to his shop.

Eh?

It's no problem. This is my factory right here.

If you'd like,

please use my umbrella.

Oh! But what will you ...

Oh my!

And so Edison met 16-year-old Mary.

It was as though his mother had sent her from heaven.

Edison and Mary were married that Christmas.

It was a quiet wedding with their families.

But even marriage couldn't change Edison,

who was so absorbed in his work that he lost track of the time.

Hey Mr. Edison, shouldn't you be on your way home?

Your wife must be waiting.

Oh no!

I'm sorry, Mary. I'll come home early tomorrow, I promise!

You're impossible!

And even after the birth of their daughter Marion...

I'm sorry, this is all we've got today.

His inventions took so much money that life was never easy for the Edisons.

......

My inventions are used by greedy companies, leaving me poor.

All my inventions do is make other people rich ...

......

Fine, then!

Edison made a momentous decision ...

I'll move my lab and produce inventions for myself!

I'll invent things that will improve the lives of everyone!

73

In 1876, Edison sold all of his property. With the money, he built a research laboratory in Menlo Park, 25 miles southwest of New York.

He began to work on a new invention in his laboratory ...

The telephone.

A, B,

C ...

I can hear it! It's faint, but I can hear it!

Good work! Keep it up!

But at that very moment, there was already someone else working on a telephone.

It was none other than Alexander Graham Bell.

Bell and Edison sent in their patent applications at nearly the same time.*

And so the Telephone War began.

*Edison's application was dated January 14, 1876, while Bell's was sent on February 14.

But Edison sent only his plans,

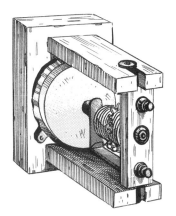

while Bell delivered the completed device. Because of this, Bell was awarded the patent.*

Ladies and gentlemen, with this great invention

I've established a telephone company.

In July 1876, Bell held a public demonstration of the telephone and became known worldwide.**

Bell's transmitter has a weak signal, and it can't carry sound very far.

Okay, then!

Never mind Bell's patent. I'm going to invent a better transmitter!

*The telephone patent dispute between Edison and Bell went to court and was not settled for 11 years.
**The demonstration was held at the Philadelphia Exposition, celebrating the 100th anniversary of the founding of the United States.

In 1877, by using grains of carbon* in the transmitter,

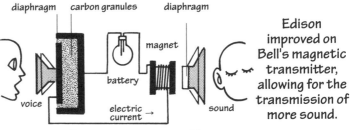

diaphragm carbon granules diaphragm

magnet

voice

battery

electric current →

sound

Edison improved on Bell's magnetic transmitter, allowing for the transmission of more sound.

① The voice moves a diaphragm, which presses on the carbon granules.

② The strength of the electric current changes with the movement of the carbon.

③ Depending on the strength of the current, a magnet touches or separates from a diaphragm, creating sound — a voice.

Hello? Hello?**

Mr. MacKenzie, can you hear me?

Yes. I can hear you!

I can hear you, my boy!

Loud and clear!

Before hitting on carbon, Edison tried about 2,000 different materials.

His notebook grew to 1,000 pages.

The Telephone War was heating up ...

*The carbon granules used in Edison's device led to the modern carbon microphone.
**Edison was the first to use "Hello" as a greeting on the telephone.

Edison invented a new type of transmitter.

Bell's company put out a new model of telephone.

But the Telephone War ended in a way no one could have predicted.

Bell's company bought the rights to everything related to the telephone.

Bell became known as the "father of the telephone."

Kruesi, could you build this for me?

Huh?

Autumn 1877: While working on the telephone, Edison had gotten an idea for yet another invention.

Um, excuse me, my boy.

Yes?

You're having Kruesi make some kind of strange device?

A machine that talks, he said ...!

Oh, that.

This is the test model here.

Let's try it out!

♪ MARY HAD A LITTLE LAMB... ♪

So it's true — the telephone war finally made him snap!

If he doesn't get some rest ...

Now we push this back —

and here we go!

♪ MARY HAD A LITTLE LAMB... ♪

WHAA?!

That machine just spoke!

How the Phonograph Works

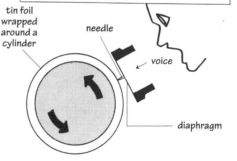

tin foil wrapped around a cylinder

needle

voice

diaphragm

① As the voice vibrates the diaphragm, the needle cuts a groove into the tin foil.

② Depending on the strength of the voice, the groove is deeper or shallower.

③ As the needle follows the groove, the diaphragm moves and the voice is reproduced.

News of the invention of the phonograph - the "talking machine" - spread throughout the country.

Mr. Edison!

Hot dogs for sale!

Edison's laboratory was flooded with people every day.

And among them was this man.

I'm Bishop John Vincent.

With God as my witness, I've come to expose your device as a sham.

It's a trick of some sort. You're using a ventriloquist or something!

Well, why don't you try recording your own voice?

Hmph!

Abaddon
Abiathar
Bezaleel
Capernaum
Ephron
Erastus
Gethsemane
Jochebed
Mahazioth
Pentateuch!*

Ha. See if you can imitate that!

Abaddon
Abiathar
Bezaleel
Capernaum
Ephron
Erastus
Gethsemane
Jochebed
Mahazioth
Pentateuch!

Ha. See if you can imitate that!

ACK!! It's really talking!

Edison even demonstrated the phonograph for U.S. President Rutherford Hayes.

Five hundred phonographs were demonstrated all over the country.

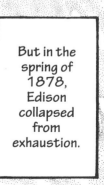

But in the spring of 1878, Edison collapsed from exhaustion.

*He was rattling off obscure names from the Bible.

That summer, Edison took a break and traveled to the Rocky Mountains.

His friend, astronomer George F. Parker, invited him to come see a solar eclipse.

Ah, it's finally beginning, Edison.

Even at noon, the sky's grown dark.

It's just like nighttime!

Look!

The Diamond Ring!*

84   *The sparkle of the portion of the sun visible from behind the moon looks just like a diamond ring.

The power of nature is truly amazing, isn't it.

Just then, an idea came to Edison for a new invention.

......

Just think how useful it would be to light up the night as though it were noon.

From this grain of an idea, the greatest invention of the century was born. Edison was 31.

Chapter 5: The Hall of Light

In 1878, the only artificial light sources besides oil lamps and candles

arc lamp

gas lamp

were the gas lamp and the arc lamp.*

The gas lamp is dangerous and smells terrible.

The arc lamp is too bright and requires a lot of electricity.

There must be a way to make a lamp that would be safe and easy to use in every household.

*The gas lamp worked by burning gas to make light. The arc lamp used the spark produced by running an electric current between two sticks of carbon.

The requirements are ...
First, it should be able to run on a voltage of around 100 volts. Second, it should be possible to turn each lamp on and off by its own switch.
Third, it should run for at least 100 hours.
Finally, it should be at a price affordable for anyone.

They seem obvious now, but these conditions were unheard-of for the time.

Um, Mr. Edison?

My name is Francis Upton. I'm starting work here today.

I'd like to know the rules of the lab and ...

Rules?

There are no rules here!

We make things here.

Otherwise, you can do as you please!

......

Now, it's time for my press briefing.

87

89

But won't you be a laughingstock if you fail?

And you'll be drowning in debt.

Worried?

If you want to quit, now's the time.

......

♪

Ha ha. He sure got you, didn't he!

Edison's the king of invention because he doesn't follow rules or common sense.

Mr. Edison!

I won't even consider quitting.

I'll stick with you to the end.

Leave all your mathematical problems to me!

It's good to have you on board, Upton.

Thank you!

Wizard of Menlo Park* Presents Plan to Electrify All of New York

Edison's plan was big news ...

and with the money he raised, he was able to get the equipment he needed for his research.

He gathered the very best talent, too ...

Upton, the master mathematician.

Ludwig Boehm, renowned glass-blower.

*"The Wizard of Menlo Park" was a popular nickname for Edison.

Charles Batchelor, a skillful technician.

And James MacKenzie and young Frank Jehl,

who always kept the lab lively.

At long last, with this talented staff,

the time had come to put everything into the invention of the electric lamp.

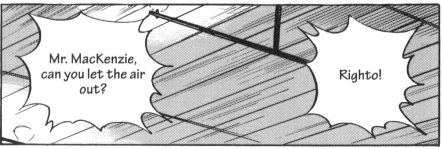

Mr. MacKenzie, can you let the air out?

Righto!

By removing the air from a glass bulb, Edison could ensure that the filament inside wouldn't burn up.*

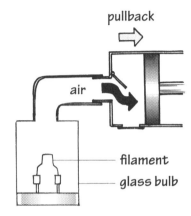

pullback

air

filament

glass bulb

PHEW! Frank, take over for me for a bit.

Yessir!

FZZT

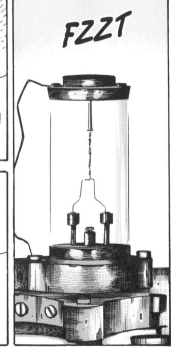

We're just about there.

Run the current.

*Filament: a wire that lights up when heated by an electric current. Creating a vacuum in the light bulb kept the hot filament from catching fire.

Ah! It lit up!

Yes! This is just right!

FZZT

Forget it. We've got to use something else.

Huh? Why?

Uh oh — it went out.

Let's see ...

So far, the platinum filament has lasted the longest.

This seems to be the limit to what we can do with platinum.

We've got to look for a material with even more electrical resistance* than platinum.

What's more, platinum is expensive,

so not everyone can afford it.

Got it.

And so the search for a new filament began.

*Edison discovered that materials with greater electrical resistance could produce light with less current.

But that doesn't mean other research was put on hold.

The lab produced many different inventions, such as the socket, the safety fuse, the switch, and various measuring instruments.

Yet, despite Edison's persistence, he couldn't find the right material for the filament.

No!

This one's a failure too.

This is the 1,600th trial, Mr. Edison.

......

Sir,

you don't suppose ...

What?

Mr. Upton wants to say, "such a material doesn't even exist!"

Right, Mr. Upton?

Wh—what are you saying, Frank?

But ... yes.

Even the newspapers are predicting we'll fail, these days.

Upton.

God wouldn't be so spiteful as to hand us a question

without an answer.

We'll find the answer.

Just as long as we don't give up.

Right, then.

Well, let's get to it.

Even this might be the answer!

Let's get to work.

Let's find the answer!

They're all exhausted from spending every night here.

Oh my.

Oh look, a button's come off.

ZZZ...

SEW

STITCH

SIGH
...

Tee hee!
He's probably
dreaming
that the
lamp's all
finished.

There —
that's
fixed.

Th—that's
it!

EEK!

Yes — I
think this
might do it!

Get up,
everyone!

There's one more
material we haven't
tried.

Nyuuh...

The carbonizing's* done.

October 21, 1879: 1:30 AM

Used #29 cotton thread.

Okay.

Let's run the current.

Yessir!

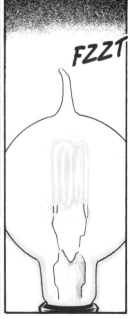

FZZT

*Carbonizing: baking an object so that it turns into carbon without burning to ash.

Ten hours later

It's still going.

We can't say it's a success until it's lasted 40 hours.

GZAWWK

Twenty hours later

I'm gonna stay up!

Frank, go to bed.

No!

Night came to Menlo Park, and then morning,

then night once again.

Finally ...

Hurrah! It's been 40 hours!

We did it! Success!

Mr. Edison, should I begin analyzing the results?

Or ...

!

Fine.

I'm going to sleep too.

Over 6,000 plants were tested as the research into filaments continued.

The result: Japanese bamboo* was found to be the best.

Edison Monument Iwashimizu Hachiman Shrine, Yawata, Kyoto, Japan

Just as he'd promised three years earlier, Edison set up a power plant and founded the Edison Illuminating Company.

Ladies and gentlemen, I shall now throw the switch!

*Bamboo grown in Yawata, Kyoto, was used for about ten years as a filament material.

Edison really is a wizard after all!

With this, I can read books even at night.

Please arrest me, officer!

With the night lit up like this, I can't be a thief anymore!

Mr. Edison.

You really are a genius.

Instead of being known as a "genius"...

I'd rather be known for my persistence.

I've worked all this time because I wanted to see this with my own eyes one day.

That's a reward in itself.

Hey, it's snowing.

This day

will remain forever in my memory.

The light bulb underwent rapid improvements,

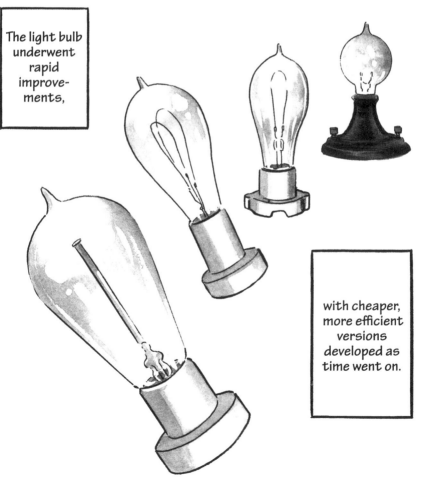

with cheaper, more efficient versions developed as time went on.

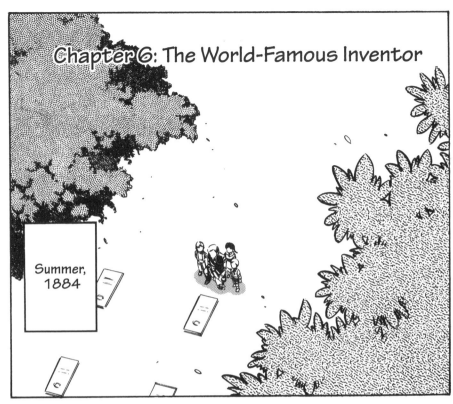

Chapter 6: The World-Famous Inventor

Summer, 1884

Well, let's be off.

Edison's wife Mary had died of typhoid fever.*

*Typhoid fever: a contagious disease that causes a high fever and internal bleeding due to intestinal bacteria.

In 1887, Edison moved the Menlo Park laboratory to West Orange.*

Perhaps his memories of life with Mary in Menlo Park were too much to bear.

Through the introduction of a concerned friend,

Edison met and married Mina Miller, 18 years younger.

Papa looks happy again!

It's about time!

*West Orange: a town in northeast New Jersey, close to New York City.

Edison began his work again with renewed vigor.

Hey Boss, what's that?

A series of photographs of a running horse. They were taken by a photographer named Muybridge.

He set up 24 cameras along a racetrack,

and as the horse broke each of the strings Muybridge had stretched across the track, one of the shutters snapped and took a photo.

If you can take a sequence of photos like this, you should be able to make them move again.

With this idea, Edison invented both the Kinetoscope (a projector) and Kinetograph (a camera).

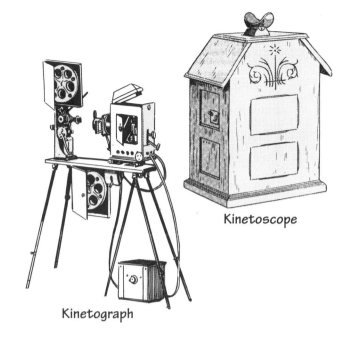

Kinetoscope

Kinetograph

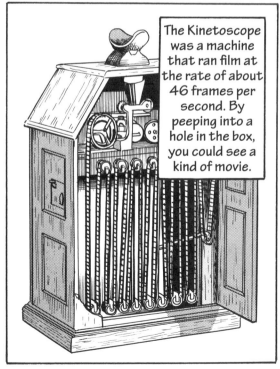

The Kinetoscope was a machine that ran film at the rate of about 46 frames per second. By peeping into a hole in the box, you could see a kind of movie.

In his Kinetoscope, Edison used the celluloid film* invented by George Eastman of Eastman Kodak Co.

*The width of this film was 35mm, the same standard size that is used today.

Edison set up the world's first movie studio* in the yard of his laboratory.

Okay, Ott, here we go.

Right.

SNIFF

SNIFF

1894: The creation of the world's first movie, "Fred Ott's Sneeze."

118   *In order to use the sun's light in the studio, the building was constructed so it could be rotated to follow the sun!

1889: The World's Fair opened in Paris, France. The Eiffel Tower was built for this occasion.

This exposition may as well have been held just for Edison.

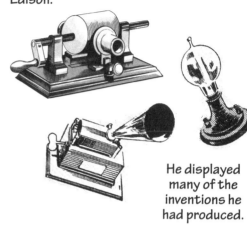

He displayed many of the inventions he had produced.

Edison was greeted with the U.S. national anthem at the Paris Opera,

and was given the highest honor from the French government, the Legion of Honor.

Edison was now truly known throughout the world.

This is all a little too much ...

At a party in 1896, Edison happened to meet a young man.

Mr. Edison!

It's a pleasure to meet you.

I'm an engineer at the Edison Illuminating Company in Detroit.

The name's Henry Ford.

This young man who so idolized Edison began telling him about his own dreams.

The age of the automobile is truly upon us.

But they've got to be made cheaper and safer.

Yes, yes.

Mr. Ford, it's a great thing to have a dream.

Don't give up on it!

At the time, Edison was doing research on electric cars.

Thank you, sir! I won't!

The young man working at Edison's company would one day be called the king of the automobile:

Henry Ford, the founder of the Ford Motor Company.

In 1908, Ford began selling the Ford Model T automobile. Mass production reduced its cost, so it was the first car cheap enough for anyone to buy.

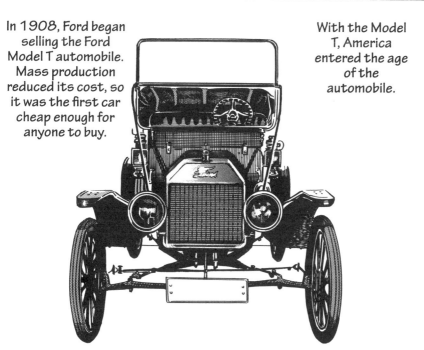

With the Model T, America entered the age of the automobile.

Despite a 16-year age difference, Ford and Edison became close friends,

and helped each others' businesses.

In 1909, Edison invented a lightweight, very efficient alkaline storage battery.*

It was immediately put to use in the Model T.

And when Edison's lab caught fire and burned to the ground,

Ford gave him an interest-free loan to rebuild it.

Edison's winter home in Florida, 1928. Edison was already 81 years old.

*An alkaline storage battery can be recharged any number of times.

Mister Edison!

How many things have you invented, now?

Ha, ha. What a question, Henry!

There are so many, I can't even count them. I have no idea.

The place that holds the most memories for you

must be Menlo Park, right?

Oh, yes.

I was so young then.

I had colleagues I could trust, and we were always so full of vim and vigor at the lab.

I was only 16 when you invented the electric light bulb.

When I read about it in the paper, I couldn't believe it.

And so I joined your company,

and now here I am enjoying a vacation with you.

It's like a dream come true for me.

How could I ever repay such a great man?

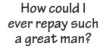

On October 21, 1929, a celebration of the 50th anniversary of the invention of the electric light bulb was held in Dearborn, Michigan.

It's an honor to have you here, Mr. Edison.

It was Henry Ford who organized the celebration.

Henry, you've outdone yourself.

There's no better gift than this.

But we've got one more

present for you.

This way.

?

Oh my ...!

125

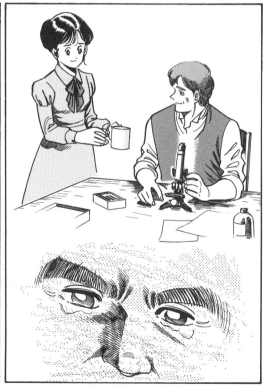

Yes, Mr. Edison?

You're ...

Eh?

Frank!!

It's really you, Frank!

It's been a long time, Mr. Edison.

That night, in his reconstructed laboratory,

Edison once again created a carbon filament light bulb.

Of course, his assistant was Frank Jehl.

Okay, Frank.

Run the current!

Yessir!

FZZT

It's lighting ...

After 50 years, in the reconstructed Menlo Park lab,

the carbon filament again glowed with a soft light.

It feels like it was only yesterday.

I am truly a fortunate man.

That night, at the party, Edison fell ill.

1931, two years later: Edison had turned 84.

His health had continued to decline,

and he only worked on his research notebook at home.

SIGH ...

I feel a little tired.

RIINGG

Hello?

Yes, this is Ford.

What?!

I see ...

On October 18, 1931, Edison died in his home.

At 1O PM on October 21, the day of the funeral ...

which happened to be the day when the first carbon filament bulb was switched on in 1879 ...

To mourn Edison's passing, lights all over America were turned off.

A moment later, the lights returned to the cities, never to be turned off again ...

Throughout Thomas Alva Edison's life, his insatiable curiosity guided everything he did.

Fearlessly investing the money he made from each invention into the next one,

undaunted by frequent setbacks, he kept moving forward to tackle new inventions.

Epilogue: Edison's Legacy

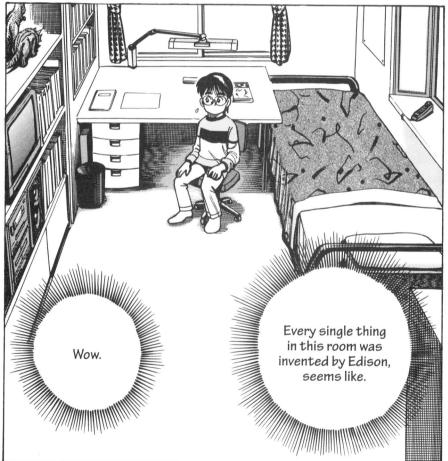

Wow.

Every single thing
in this room was
invented by Edison,
seems like.

142

Edison left us with many wise sayings.

And every one was based on the truth of his own experience.

Let's end with one of those quotes.

"Genius is
one percent
inspiration and
ninety-nine
percent
perspiration."

Thomas
Alva Edison

Thomas Edison On the Map

This map shows the locations of important events in the life of Thomas Edison.

❶   Order of events
➔14   Related page in story

Stratford, Ontario
   ❹ 1864: Becomes a train
     station telegraph
     operator. ➔ 40

Lake Erie

Port Huron, Michigan
   ❷ 1862: Begins selling
     his own newspaper,
     The Weekly Herald,
     on the train. ➔ 16

Milan, Ohio
❶ 1847: Born on February 11.
   ➔ 24

Mount Clemens, Michigan
   ❸ 1862: Learns telegraphy
     from the stationmaster after
     saving his son's life. ➔ 39

Dearborn, Michigan
⓯ 1929: Honored at a celebration of
the 50th anniversary of his invention of the light bulb. ➔ 125

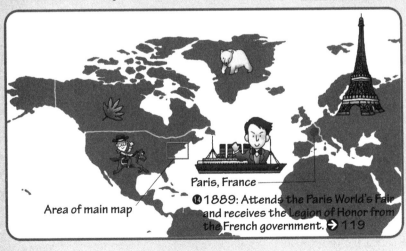

Area of main map

Paris, France
⓮ 1889: Attends the Paris World's Fair
and receives the Legion of Honor from
the French government. ➔ 119

146

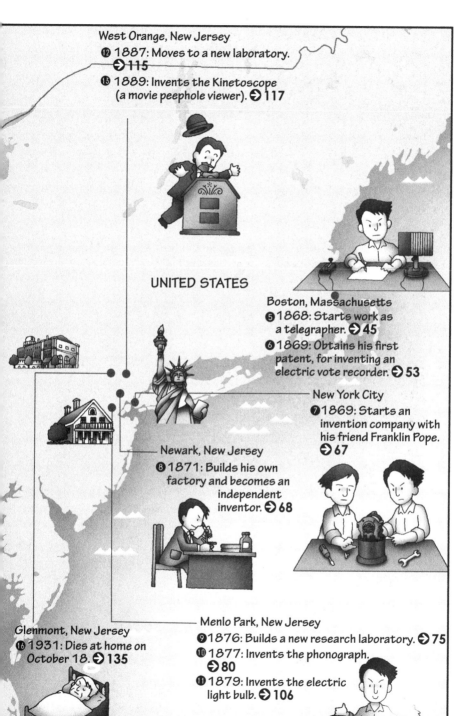

West Orange, New Jersey
⑫ 1887: Moves to a new laboratory.
⊘115

⑬ 1889: Invents the Kinetoscope
(a movie peephole viewer). **⊘117**

UNITED STATES

Boston, Massachusetts
⑤ 1868: Starts work as
a telegrapher. **⊘45**

⑥ 1869: Obtains his first
patent, for inventing an
electric vote recorder. **⊘53**

New York City
⑦ 1869: Starts an
invention company with
his friend Franklin Pope.
⊘67

Newark, New Jersey
⑧ 1871: Builds his own
factory and becomes an
independent
inventor. **⊘68**

Glenmont, New Jersey
⑯ 1931: Dies at home on
October 18. **⊘135**

Menlo Park, New Jersey
⑨ 1876: Builds a new research laboratory. **⊘75**

⑩ 1877: Invents the phonograph.
⊘80

⑪ 1879: Invents the electric
light bulb. **⊘106**

147

Timeline: The Life of Thomas Edison

Year	Age	Event
1847	0	February 11: Born in Milan, Ohio, USA to Nancy and Samuel Edison.
1854	7	July: Family moves to Port Huron, Michigan.
1855	8	Enters grade school, but is taken out after three months to be tutored at home by his mother.
1859	12	Begins selling newspapers on the Grand Trunk Railway.
		Sets up a laboratory in the baggage car of a train and conducts chemistry experiments.
1862	15	Begins selling his own newspaper, *The Weekly Herald*, on the train.
		Saves the stationmaster's son from being hit by a train at Mount Clemens station. In gratitude, the stationmaster, J.U. MacKenzie, teaches him telegraphy.
1864	17	Takes a job as night telegraph operator at Stratford Junction, Ontario, Canada.
1868	21	Starts work as a telegrapher at the Western Union telegraph office in Boston.
1869	22	June: Obtains his first patent, for the invention of an electric vote recorder.

Year	Age	Event
		Moves to New York City and is hired by the Gold and Stock Reporting Telegraph Company.
		October: Starts a company with his friend Franklin Pope and invents the Gold Printer.
1871	24	Builds his own factory in Newark, New Jersey.
		Invents the Edison Universal Stock Printer, which includes a forerunner of the electric typewriter.
		Mother Nancy dies.
		Marries Mary Stillwell.
1876	29	Builds a new research laboratory in Menlo Park, New Jersey.
1877	30	Invents a carbon transmitter for the telephone. Invents the phonograph.
		Demonstrates the phonograph for U.S. President Rutherford B. Hayes at the White House.
1878	31	Begins research on an incandescent electric lamp.
1879	32	October 21: Invents the first successful electric light bulb using a long-lasting carbon filament.

149

Timeline: The Life of Thomas Edison

Year	Age	Event
1880	33	Patents various inventions related to electric lighting, including sockets and switches.
		Begins research on electric trains.
		Fails in his experiments with a flying machine.
		Invents a method of iron ore separation using a magnet.
1882	35	Builds the world's first electric power stations in London and New York.
1883	36	Discovers the "Edison Effect" of electrons emitted from a light bulb filament, later applied to the vacuum tubes used in radios.
1884	37	Wife Mary dies.
1885	38	Obtains a patent for wireless communication.
1886	39	Marries Mina Miller.
1887	40	Moves his laboratory to West Orange, New Jersey.
		Begins making improvements to the cylinder phonograph.
1889	42	Invents the Kinetoscope (a movie peephole viewer) and Kinetograph (a movie camera).

Year	Age	Event
		Attends the Paris World's Fair amid much fanfare.
1894	47	Invents a movie projector and builds the world's first movie studio. Begins marketing movie projectors for home use.
1896	49	Meets Henry Ford.
1898	51	Invents a method of building houses with concrete.
1909	62	Invents an alkaline storage battery.
1913	66	Invents the Kinetophone, which combines the Kinetoscope with a phonograph.
1929	82	Invents a method of extracting rubber from the goldenrod plant.
		October 21: A celebration of the 50th anniversary of the invention of the electric light bulb is held in Dearborn, Michigan.
		Henry Ford reconstructs the Menlo Park Laboratory and presents it to Edison at the celebration (it is now part of the Edison Institute museum complex in Dearborn).
1931	84	October 18: Dies at Glenmont, his estate in West Orange, New Jersey.